W0291242

Abschlussprüfung

Englisch

Jahrgangsstufe 10
Brandenburg

Cornelsen

Abschlussprüfung Englisch, Jahrgangsstufe 10, Brandenburg

Erarbeitet von:	David Christie, Banbury, u.a.
Beratung:	Birgit Estabillo, Berlin
Redaktion:	Anja Zieschang, Doreen Arnold (Assistenz)
Umschlaggestaltung:	havemannundmosch, Konzeption und Gestaltung, Berlin
Layout und technische Umsetzung:	Yvonne Thron, Berlin

Illustrationen:
Roland Beier, Berlin (SF: Illustrationen); **Gareth Evans**, Berlin (SF Talking about charts: Diagramm unten); **Jeongsook Lee**, Heidelberg (S.37; 38; 41; 42; 55; 56; 61; 66); **Karin Mall**, Berlin (SF Talking about charts: Diagramme oben u. Mitte)

Bildquellen:
Alamy, Abingdon (S.12 unten (u. 14): Janine Wiedel Photolibrary; S.16: VStock (RF); S. 20: Janine Wiedel Photolibrary; S.22: Jim West; S.25: Robert Harding Picture Library Ltd.; S.30: Friedrich Stark; S.31 oben: Friedrich Stark; S.34: allOver photography; SF Describing pictures, landscape: Horizon International Images Limited, boy: Beyond Fotomedia GmbH (RF); S.43: Bubbles Photolibrary; S.46 (u. 48): ACE STOCK LIMITED; S.47 oben (u. 49): vario images GmbH & Co. KG, unten (u. 49): John Powell Photographer; S.50 oben: David J. Green – Lifestyle; S.53 li.: Comstock Premium (RF), re.: Topix (RF); S.60: Dinodia Photos; S.62 re. (M): Images North; S.63: Janine Wiedel Photolibrary; S.65 unten: imagebroker; S.75 oben: Picture Contact BV; S.76: PCL; S.77 oben: Image Source (RF), unten: Danita Delimont; S.79: Photofusion Picture Library); **CartoonStock**, Bath (S.12 oben (u. 14): Aaron Bacall; S.32 oben: John Morris, unten: Shannon Burns; S.33: Len Hawkins; S.67: Wilbur -Dawbarn-; S.68 oben: Tim Cordell, unten: Ron Morgan); **Corbis**, Düsseldorf (S.23 unten: Ocean; S.26: Maria (M): PictureNet (RF), tenements (M): Photo Collection Alexander Alland, Sr., Larry (M): Royalty-Free, immigrants (M): Bettmann; SF Titelbild: Patrick Giardino); **ecopix Fotoagentur**, Berlin (S.57 oben: ecopix Fotoagentur); **Financial Times**, London (SF Describing cartoons: Ingram Pinn); **Fotoagentur VISUM**, Hamburg (S.28: Jo Holz); **Getty Images**, München (S.24; S.57 unten: Steffen A. Jakob; S.73); **iStockphoto**, Calgary (S.9: Csondy; S.19 oben: LeggNet, unten: timegoodwin; S.21 oben: RapidEye; S.27 li.: phildate; S.65 oben: apomares; S.74: gchutka); **Picture Alliance**, Frankfurt/Main (S.59 oben: dpa, unten: dpa/dpa-web); **Shutterstock**, New York (S.7: Kuzma; S.10 li.: linerpics, re.: Gina Sanders; S.11: stefanolunardi; S.13 (u. 15): Smart7 / Shutterstock.com; S.17 li. u. re.: Monkey Business Images; S. 21 unten: Geoffrey Kuchera / Shutterstock.com; S.23 oben: Natursports / Shutterstock.com; S.27 Mitte: ilolab, re.: Vladimir Nikulin; S.29 oben: Philip Lange, unten: TheSupe87; S.31 unten: fstockfoto / Shutterstock.com; S.35: Elzbieta Sekowska; S.36: Alistair Scott; S.39 oben: Kurhan, unten: Bobby Deal / RealDealPhoto; S.40: stefanolunardi; S.44: LiveStock; S.50 unten: MANDY GODBEHEAR; S.51: Monkey Business Images; S.52: Jetrel; S.58: Dianne Maire / Shutterstock.com; S.62 li. (M): claudia veja; S.72: Val Thoermer; S.75 unten: Kiselev Andrey Valerevich; S.78 oben: Marcin Balcerzak, unten: Morgan Lane Photography)

Titelbild:
Corbis, Düsseldorf (cyclist green helmet (M): Motofish Images; cyclist red helmet (M): Patrick Giardino); **Getty Images**, München (window (M): Bryan Mullennix); **iStockphoto**, Calgary (Capitol (M): Cheng Chang)

www.cornelsen.de

1. Auflage, 1. Druck 2011

© 2011 Cornelsen Verlag, Berlin

Das Werk und seine Teile sind urheberrechtlich geschützt.
Jede Nutzung in anderen als den gesetzlich zugelassenen Fällen bedarf der vorherigen schriftlichen Einwilligung des Verlages.
Hinweis zu den §§ 46, 52 a UrhG: Weder das Werk noch seine Teile dürfen ohne eine solche Einwilligung eingescannt und in ein Netzwerk eingestellt oder sonst öffentlich zugänglich gemacht werden.
Dies gilt auch für Intranets von Schulen und sonstigen Bildungseinrichtungen.

Druck: CS-Druck CornelsenStürtz, Berlin

ISBN 978-3-06-032289-3

Inhalt gedruckt auf säurefreiem Papier aus nachhaltiger Forstwirtschaft.

INHALT

Liebe Schülerin, lieber Schüler!

Dieses Heft hilft dir, dich auf die Prüfung am Ende der Jahrgangsstufe 10 im Fach Englisch vorzubereiten. Du findest hier Übungsmaterialien geordnet nach allen Themen des *Rahmenlehrplans für moderne Fremdsprachen* für die schriftliche und mündliche Prüfung im Fach Englisch auf den drei Anforderungsniveaus: erweiterter Hauptschulabschluss / die erweiterte Berufsbildungsreife (EBR); Realschulabschluss / Fachoberschulreife (FOR); Berechtigung zum Besuch der gymnasialen Oberstufe (GOST). Die Übungen für die einzelnen Anforderungsniveaus sind jeweils im Heft gekennzeichnet.

Die Prüfung im Überblick

Die Prüfung am Ende der Jahrgangsstufe 10 testet in der schriftlichen Prüfung das Hörverstehen und in der mündlichen Prüfung ausschließlich die fremdsprachliche Handlungsfähigkeit, d.h. die spontane Kommunikation in der Fremdsprache.

Die schriftliche Prüfung in Englisch dauert 45 Minuten. Sie wird für alle Anforderungsniveaus an einem zentral festgelegten Tag durchgeführt. Alle Schüler sind verpflichtet, diese schriftliche Prüfung im Fach Englisch zu absolvieren, die mit 20 % in die Prüfungsnote eingeht.

Die mündliche Prüfung besteht aus drei Teilen und dauert abhängig von der Gruppengröße (2–3 Schüler) insgesamt 15–20 Minuten. Es gibt keine Vorbereitungszeit.

Aufgaben in der schriftlichen Prüfung

Die schriftlichen Aufgaben können von Jahr zu Jahr unterschiedlich sein. Einige Aufgabentypen kommen jedoch sehr oft vor. In diesem Heft wirst du nicht nur diese typischen Aufgaben finden, sondern auch andere mögliche Prüfungsaufgaben. Wenn du mit diesem Heft arbeitest, wirst du für deine Prüfung gut vorbereitet sein.

1 *True, False*-Aufgaben

True/False (richtig oder falsch) bzw. *Yes/No* Fragen sind sehr häufig in den Listening-Teilen anzutreffen. Hier ist ein Beispiel: Eine amerikanische *high school*-Schülerin berichtet, dass ihre Schule 500 Schüler und Schülerinnen umfasst und dass sie ihre Schule sehr gerne mag. In der Prüfung sieht die Aufgabe dann so aus:

		True (Yes)	False (No)
1	There are 500 pupils at Carol's school.	✓	
2	Carol hates her school.		✓

Diese Fragen werden immer wie oben beantwortet, indem du einen Haken im richtigen Kästchen setzt. Häufig lautet die Überschrift: *Listen and put a tick (✓) in the (correct) box.*

2 *Multiple Choice*-Aufgaben (Mehrfach-Wahl-Antworten)

In einer *Multiple Choice*-Aufgabe musst du die richtige Antwort aus mehreren möglichen Antworten heraussuchen. Meistens mit dem Zusatz: *There is only one correct answer for each question.* Beispiel: Eine Freundin aus England berichtet über ihr Wochenende. Dir wird die Frage gestellt:

1 What did Sandy do last weekend?

A ☐ visited a friend **B** ☐ went swimming **C** ✓ saw a film

Die richtige Antwort der drei möglichen ist **C** und wird mit einem Haken markiert.

3 Andere Aufgaben in den *Listening*-Teilen

Eine Art von Aufgabe, die dir in der Prüfung begegnen könnte, ist eine Zuordnungsaufgabe *(Matching)*. Beispiel: Ein Text handelt von fünf Jugendlichen – was sie gerne machen, wie viel Geld sie zur Verfügung haben etc. Dir werden Aussagen (A–F) präsentiert und du musst jedem Jugendlichen die passende Aussage zuordnen. Egal welche Art von Aufgabe drankommt, sie wird genau erklärt. Beachte die Aufgabenstellung, dann wirst du keine Probleme mit den Anforderungen haben.

Aufgaben in der mündlichen Prüfung

Die mündliche Prüfung wird von 2–3 Schülern/Schülerinnen gleichzeitig absolviert. Die Prüfung besteht aus folgenden Aufgaben:

- Part 1 (Dauer ca. 4–6 Min.) dient als *warming-up*, um dir den Einstieg in die fremdsprachliche Kommunikation zu erleichtern: Dein Englischlehrer / deine Englischlehrerin wird jedem einzelnen Prüfling abwechselnd vier bis sechs Fragen stellen, die thematisch dem ersten Thema des Rahmenlehrplans *Familie – Freunde – Wertvorstellungen* entsprechen.
- Part 2 (Dauer ca. 5–7 Min.): Jeder Prüfling bekommt vom Englischlehrer / von der Englischlehrerin einen Bildimpuls (z. B. Foto, Cartoon, Grafik) mit einer Aufgabenstellung. Deren Inhalt ist hauptsächlich auf die Bildbeschreibung ausgerichtet sowie auf eine allgemeine Interpretation des Bildes oder aber auf das Beantworten von Fragen. Die Bildimpulse entsprechen thematisch einem Thema des Rahmenlehrplans.
- Part 3 (Dauer ca. 6–7 Min.) greift das Thema der Bildimpulse aus dem zweiten Teil auf. Dein Englischlehrer / deine Englischlehrerin beschreibt eine Situation, die dann von dir und den anderen Prüflingen diskutiert wird.

Einige Tipps

Dieses Heft bietet dir viele nützliche Übungen, um dich auf deine Prüfung vorzubereiten. Wenn du darüber hinaus dein Englisch auffrischen möchtest, solltest du folgende Elemente in deinem Englisch-Plan berücksichtigen:

Aufbau des Vokabulars

Der schönste Gedanke nützt nichts, wenn dir das Vokabular fehlt, um ihn auszudrücken. Man unterscheidet zwischen aktivem (Wörter, die man selbst anwendet) und passivem (Wörter, die man versteht, aber nicht anwendet) Vokabular.

a) **Passives zu aktivem Vokabular machen.** Lies/Höre Texte bewusst daraufhin, welche Wörter du verstehst. Schreibe die Wörter auf und benutze sie im Unterricht / in der Freizeit.

b) **Mäßig, aber regelmäßig üben.** Mehr als 10–15 Ausdrücke pro Übungsphase merkt man sich normalerweise nicht. Lerne also immer wieder kleinere Einheiten statt endlose Listen.

c) **In Wortfeldern arbeiten.** Wähle ein Thema, z. B. den Handlungsverlauf deines Lieblingsfilms. Entwirf eine Mindmap zum Thema. Schreibe die englischen Begriffe hinein. Schlage fehlende Begriffe im Wörterbuch nach (auch die Aussprache). Überprüfe, mit welchen Präpositionen und in welchem Kontext die Ausdrücke eingesetzt werden. Lerne die neuen Ausdrücke. Versuche in der nächsten Vokabelübungsphase einen kurzen Text zum Thema zu schreiben und möglichst viele der neuen Vokabeln zu verwenden.

d) **In Zusammenhängen lernen.** Suche nach Wortfamilien, Gegensatz- und Synonympaaren. Alles, was Struktur bringt, hilft dir.

e) **Mit Methode lernen.** Welcher Lerntyp bist du?

- Du lernst über die Ohren: Nimm Vokabeln und Beispielsätze auf und höre sie dir auf dem Weg zur Schule an.
- Du lernst über die Augen: Schreibe Vokabeln mehrmals, gestalte ein „Lernbild" und hänge es neben den Spiegel. So kannst du die Wörter beim Zähneputzen wiederholen.
- Du lernst durch Organisieren und Sortieren: Arbeite mit Karteikarten. Sortiere und gruppiere Vokabeln immer wieder um.

Auffüllen von Lücken

Fertige sorgfältige Korrekturen deiner Klassenarbeiten und Tests an und arbeite an deinen Fehlerschwerpunkten:

a) Schau dir die Grammatik in deinem Englischbuch noch einmal an.

b) Schau dir dein Wörterbuch genau an. Es enthält auch Übungsseiten zu besonderen Problemen des Englischen.

c) Arbeite so lange an einem Problem, bis es beseitigt ist. Vergisst du z.B. stets das *third person -s*, schreibe und spreche so lange Texte mit diesem Schwerpunkt, bis du diesen Fehler nicht mehr machst, bevor du dich um das nächste Problem kümmerst.

d) Sprich im Unterricht konsequent Englisch und bitte deinen Übungspartner / deine Übungspartnerin besonders auf deine Fehlerschwerpunkte zu achten.

Spaß-Englisch

Tauche in die englische Sprache ein – die beste, spaßigste und effektivste Lernmethode.

a) Schau Filme auf DVD in Englisch mit englischen Untertiteln.

b) Versuche so weit als möglich den Text deiner Lieblingslieder beim Hören zu verstehen und dann zu übersetzen.

c) Lies englische Lektüren. Dabei zählen nur zwei Dinge: Die Lektüre soll Spaß machen und darf nicht zu schwer sein. Falls du Schwierigkeiten mit der Aussprache hast, besorge dir das Buch als Hörbuch. Vieles findet sich auch in Bibliotheken.

d) Das Internet ist eine wahre Fundgrube. Suche nach deinen Interessensgebieten auf Englisch.

Mach das Beste aus deiner Note. Die mündliche Beteiligung macht mehr als die Hälfte der Gesamtnote aus. Nimm dir vor, dich in einer Stunde mindestens fünf Mal zu melden und führe eine Strichliste, um zu prüfen, ob du das auch einhältst. Stelle deine Hausaufgaben vor oder nimm Präsentationsmöglichkeiten wahr.

Wir wünschen dir viel Erfolg für deine Prüfung!

1 Familie – Freunde – Wertvorstellungen

EBR Listening: Party plans

- *Tom is planning a party.*
- *He's phoning his new friend Sabine. Sabine's family moved to England two months ago.*
- *Read the table below first, then listen to the recording.*
- *Complete the table.*
- *You will hear the recording twice.*

Listen to the telephone conversation and fill in the table – as you listen.

Village	
Street	
House number	

Name	
Time (Numbers, please!)	p.m.
Phone number	

FOR Listening: An internet magazine

- *Laura is a 10th grade student at a high school in Wisconsin.*
- *She is talking about the German lessons in her class.*
- *Read tasks 1–6 below first, then listen to the recording.*
- *Tick (✓) the correct answer: A, B or C.*
- *You will hear the recording twice.*

1 Laura's German class started the internet magazine project

A ☐ six months ago.

B ☐ three months ago.

C ☐ last year.

2 The project is with a school in

A ☐ Dresden.

B ☐ Dusseldorf.

C ☐ Berlin.

3 All the articles in the magazine are in

A ☐ English.

B ☐ German.

C ☐ German and English.

4 Laura thinks that the most interesting articles in the magazine are about

A ☐ the two towns where the pupils live.

B ☐ the different sports the pupils like.

C ☐ the different food the pupils eat.

5 Laura made a video for the magazine. In the video she

A ☐ sang a song.

B ☐ talked about her hobbies.

C ☐ interviewed some teachers at her school.

6 Laura's magazine

A ☐ is on the internet now.

B ☐ will perhaps be on the internet in three months from now.

C ☐ will perhaps be on the internet next year.

GOST Listening: Marriages in England and Wales

- *You are going to hear an interview with Claire Strongboard, a professor of relationship studies.*
- *She is talking about marriages in England and Wales.*
- *Read tasks 1–6 below first, then listen to the recording.*
- *Tick (✓) the correct answer: A, B or C.*
- *You will hear the recording twice.*

1 According to Claire the number of marriages has declined because

A ☐ women today don't find potential husbands.

B ☐ women today can make a good living for themselves.

C ☐ women today think that marriage is just a piece of paper.

2 As recently as twenty years ago women

A ☐ had a good quality of life.

B ☐ had many opportunities.

C ☐ had to care for their family and their home.

3 According to Claire people today

A ☐ think they can't afford to get married.

B ☐ think they can't afford to get divorced.

C ☐ think they can't afford to pay their partner money.

4 Ruth

A ☐ thinks it's very easy to get married today.

B ☐ got divorced and doesn't want to get married anymore.

C ☐ doesn't understand why people get married.

5 Before she gets married, Lucy

A ☐ wants to finish university and get a job.

B ☐ wants to get a bit older.

C ☐ wants to find a good potential husband.

6 Frank thinks that

A ☐ lots of British people like marriage.

B ☐ the number of marriages is very low in Britain.

C ☐ young people are not interested in getting married.

EBR Speaking: A new home

Part 1

Please answer the questions about yourself.

- *Where exactly do you live? How long have you lived there?*
- *Do you have any brothers or sisters? What are their names?*
- *Do you have any pets?*

Part 2

Teacher: I'm going to give each of you a photograph which shows people moving house. Candidate A, please show your photograph to the other candidates. Describe the photograph and talk about your experiences of moving house. Have you ever moved house or helped someone move?

Candidate A

Candidate B

Teacher: Candidate B, please show your photograph to the other candidates. Describe the photograph and talk about where your first own flat should be and what it should be like?

Teacher: Candidate C, please show your photograph to the other candidates and say what you can see in the picture. Talk about who you would like to share your first flat with? Or would you prefer to live on your own?

Candidate C

Part 3

Teacher: Now I'd like you to have a discussion. Would you like to move to another town or city after you have finished school? Discuss the chances and the problems.

FOR Speaking: Life as a teenager

Part 1

Please answer the questions about yourself.

- *Who do you live with?*
- *Where does the rest of your family live?*
- *Do you often see your extended family? Why (not)?*
- *Who in your family are you very close to? Why?*

Part 2

Teacher: I'm going to give each of you a picture which shows young people in different situations. Candidate A, show the cartoon to the other candidates and describe it. What is the teacher's problem?

Candidate A

"Must you keep reminding me by wearing that shirt?"

Candidate B

Teacher: Candidate B, show the photo to the other candidates. Describe the picture and talk about where you and your friends meet and what you do.

Candidate C

Teacher: Candidate C, show the photo to the other candidates and describe it. Have you ever protested about something? What was it and what did you do?

Part 3

Teacher: Now I'd like you to have a discussion. Some older people say that young people today are lazy and don't know what to do with their lives. Do you agree or disagree? Give examples to support your opinion.

GOST Speaking: Young people today and tomorrow

Part 1

Please answer the questions about yourself.
- *Where do you and your friends meet in the afternoon? What do you do?*
- *Who do you live with? Where does the rest of your family live?*
- *Who is your favourite family member? Why?*

Part 2

Teacher: I'm going to give each of you a picture which shows young people in different situations. Candidate A, show the cartoon to the other candidates and describe it. Explain the problem the cartoon shows.

Candidate A

"Must you keep reminding me by wearing that shirt?"

Candidate B

Teacher: Candidate B, show the photo to the other candidates. Describe the picture and talk about your attitude towards teenagers who hang around in shopping centres or in the street.

Teacher: Candidate C, show the photo to the other candidates and describe it. What do you know about student demonstrations in Germany in the past and today?

Candidate C

Part 3

Teacher: Now I'd like you to have a discussion. What will the future of today's young generation look like? Here are some ideas you might want to consider:

- education
- jobs
- family
- …

2 Bildung – Politik – Wirtschaft

EBR Listening: Your English is fantastic

- *Jack is an apprentice[1] from Yorkshire in the north of England. Marco is an apprentice from Essen in Germany.*
- *Jack is staying with Marco's family for a week.*
- *You are going to hear a conversation between Jack and Marco.*
- *Read tasks 1–5 below first, then listen to the recording.*
- *Tick (✓) the correct answer: A, B or C.*
- *You will hear the recording twice.*

1 What does Jack think about Marco's English?

A ☐ It's OK.

B ☐ Marco makes lots of mistakes.

C ☐ It's fantastic.

2 Where does Marco learn English now?

A ☐ At home with some CDs.

B ☐ At school.

C ☐ At college.

3 Jack says that Marco's family is

A ☐ "really cool".

B ☐ "really friendly".

C ☐ "really big".

4 What did Jack think about the meal they had yesterday evening?

A ☐ He didn't like it so much.

B ☐ It was his favourite meal so far.

C ☐ He liked some of it.

5 After their conversation, Jack and Marco are going to

A ☐ go swimming.

B ☐ go shopping.

C ☐ go canoeing.

1 ***apprentice*** *Lehrling*

FOR Listening: How teenagers spend their money

- *Two friends, Alice and Kevin are talking about how they spend their pocket money.*
- *Read questions A–H below first, then listen to the recording.*
- *Write the correct letters in Kevin's and Alice's box.*
- *You will hear the recording twice.*

Who

A ... goes to the cinema and buys popcorn?

B ... is saving £10 a month?

C ... gets £5 a week?

D ... wants to get a job?

E ... earns money for babysitting?

F ... buys video games?

G ... never has any money?

H ... gets £20 a month?

Kevin

☐ ☐ ☐ ☐

Alice

☐ ☐ ☐ ☐

GOST Listening: School election

- *You are going to hear a radio interview about a school election at a college in South London.*
- *Read the statements 1–6 below first, then listen to the recording.*
- *Complete the statements.*
- *You will hear the recording twice.*

1 Chris is one of the ______________________________.

2 Three groups of students at Oldfield College represent ______________________________

______________________________.

3 Besides having meetings and debates the students will ______________________________

______________________________ in lunch breaks.

4 Jenny thinks it's a shame that ______________________________.

5 According to Chris the school election is a chance for students to ______________________________

______________________________.

6 Chris thinks the situation at the school election is quite ______________________________

______________________________.

EBR Speaking: Homeless people

Part 1

Please answer the questions about yourself.

- *What are your favourite subjects at school?*
- *How did you get to school today?*
- *Do you or your family have a good relationship with your neighbours? What are your neighbours like?*

Part 2

Candidate A

Teacher: I'm going to give each of you a picture which shows poor people. Candidate A, show the photo to the other candidates and describe it. Are there homeless people in your area, too?

Teacher: Candidate B, show the photo to the other candidates. Describe the picture and talk about what homeless people in Germany can do if they need help.

Candidate B

Teacher: Candidate C, show the photo to the other candidates and describe it. Talk about how people can become homeless.

Candidate C

Part 3

Teacher: Now I'd like you to describe to each other what you can do to help homeless people in Germany. Here are some ideas:

- Help in a food kitchen.
- Volunteer for community service.
- Collect/Donate money/clothes.
- ...

FOR Speaking: Volunteers

Part 1

Please answer the questions about yourself.

- *What do you like about school?*
- *Do you do any activities besides school? What do you do?*
- *Have you ever helped someone in the street? What did you do?*
- *Do you want to have children one day? Why (not)?*

Part 2

Candidate A

Teacher: I'm going to give each of you a picture which shows volunteers. Candidate A, show the photo to the other candidates and describe it. Talk about what you or your family have done or do to help people in need.

Candidate B

Teacher: Candidate B, show the photo to the other candidates and describe the picture. Talk about other kinds of volunteer work that you know.

Teacher: Candidate C, show the photo to the other candidates. Describe the picture and tell us what you think about volunteer work.

Candidate C

Useful vocabulary:

food kitchen Suppenküche

Part 3

Teacher: Now I'd like you to have a discussion. More and more people take a year off after school to do volunteer work. They work with children or help disabled people, for example. Decide whether or not you would take a year off to do volunteer work. Give reasons for your decisions.

GOST Speaking: Elections

Part 1

Please answer the questions about yourself.

- *How do you get information about what's going on in Germany and the world?*
- *Are you interested in politics? Why (not)?*
- *What should your future life look like? Where would you be? What would you do?*

Part 2

Candidate A

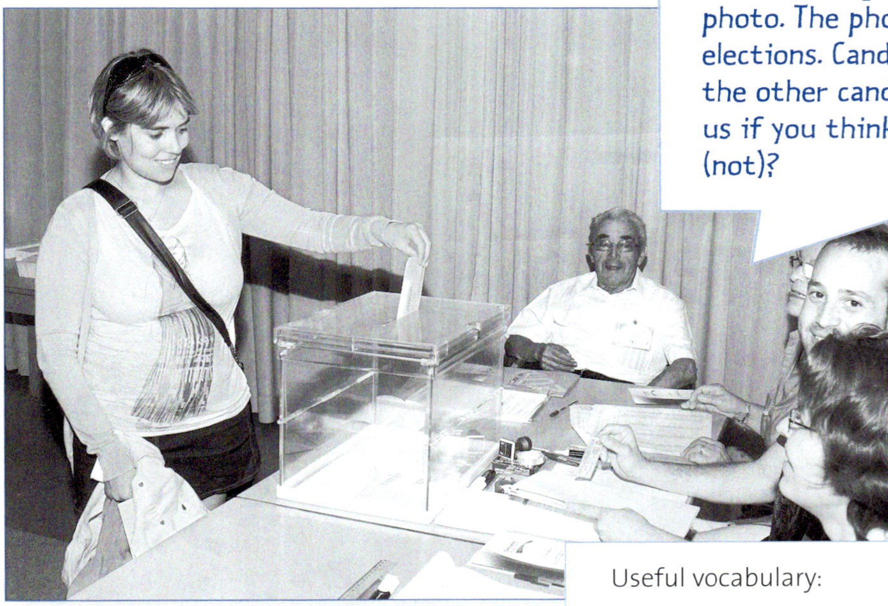

Teacher: I'm going to give each of you a photo. The photos show politicians and elections. Candidate A, show the photo to the other candidates. Describe it and tell us if you think voting is important. Why (not)?

Useful vocabulary:

ballot box	*Wahlurne*
election worker	*Wahlhelfer*
election office	*Wahlbüro*
election campaign	*Wahlkampagne*

Candidate B

Teacher: Candidate B, show the photo to the other candidates and describe the picture. Tell us what politicians in Germany do during their election campaigns.

Teacher: Candidate C, show the photo to the other candidates and describe it. Does the political situation influence your life? How?

Candidate C

Part 3

Teacher: Now I'd like you to have a discussion. In some German federal states the voting age for local elections is 16. Discuss whether the voting age should be lowered to 16 for all public elections in Germany. What are the pros and cons?

3 Vergangenheit – Gegenwart – Zukunft

EBR Listening: A flying doctor in Australia

- *You are going to hear a flying doctor talking about his work in Australia.*
- *Read tasks 1–6 below first and look at the useful vocabulary. Then listen to the recording.*
- *Tick (✓) the correct answer: A, B or C.*
- *You will hear the recording twice.*

Useful vocabulary:

internet addict	*Internetsüchtige(r)*
missionary	*Missionar/in*
development	*Entwicklung*
nearby	*in der Nähe*
aircraft	*Flugzeug*

1 John started work as a flying doctor
- A ☐ thirty years ago.
- B ☐ fifteen years ago.
- C ☐ five years ago.

2 How many Australians live in the Outback?
- A ☐ 10 percent.
- B ☐ A few.
- C ☐ Most.

3 Who was "Flynn of the Outback"?
- A ☐ A pilot.
- B ☐ A missionary.
- C ☐ A radio technician.

4 What was necessary for the development of the Service?
- A ☐ Radios and aeroplanes.
- B ☐ Hospitals and doctors.
- C ☐ Towns and cities.

5 How many aircraft does the Service have today?
- A ☐ More than 50.
- B ☐ Less than 50.
- C ☐ More than 15.

6 John says every day is
- A ☐ routine.
- B ☐ long.
- C ☐ different.

FOR Listening: Coming to America

- *You are going to hear four people talking about immigrating to the United States.*
- *Read the statements A–H below first, then listen to the recording.*
- *Choose the correct statements.*
- *There are two statements for each person.*
- *Write the correct letters in the spaces.*
- *You will hear the recording twice.*

A There are some things I miss from my home country.

B There were ten of us living in two rooms.

C I saw thousands of people in the Immigration Building.

D People were interested in me because I was from another country.

E My brother and sister were too old to come with us.

F We were worried they wouldn't let us in.

G We were shocked at how dirty everything was.

H My mom is not completely happy here.

Person	Statement
Larry	
Maria	
Miriam	
Fali	

Maria

Larry

GOST Listening: Working in the outback

- *You are going to listen to a reporter interviewing three young people who work in the Australian outback.*
- *Read the questions A–I below first, then listen to the recording.*
- *Write the correct letters in Robert's, Rachel's or Cora's box.*
- *You will hear the recording twice.*

Who

A ... works for two weeks in a row?

B ... likes talking to people?

C ... teaches children about a different culture?

D ... likes to go to the beach?

E ... works at a very special place?

F ... meets native Australians?

G ... spends time in a nice and cool environment?

H ... knows about animals in the outback?

I ... does really hard work?

Robert

Rachel

Cora

EBR Speaking: A day in Berlin

Part 1

Please answer the questions about yourself.

- *Have you ever been to a foreign country? Where have you been and when?*
- *Which country would you like to visit one day? What would you like to do there?*
- *Do you know people from abroad? Where are they from?*

Part 2

Candidate A

Teacher: I'm going to give each of you a photograph of Berlin. Candidate A, show the photo to the other candidates. Describe it and talk about a tourist tour you did during your holidays. Where was the tour and what was it like?

Candidate B

Teacher: Candidate B, show the photo to the other candidates. Describe the picture and talk about other sights in Berlin. What do you know about them?

Candidate C

Teacher: Candidate C, show the photo to the other candidates. Describe the picture and talk about a concert you have been to. What was it like?

Part 3

Teacher: Now I'd like you to have a discussion. You are going to be in Berlin for one day. Discuss what you want to do there and which sights you want to see.

FOR Speaking: Johannesburg

Part 1

Please answer the questions about yourself.
- *What's your favourite country? Why?*
- *Do you know people from abroad? Where did you meet them?*
- *Have you ever been to a foreign country? Where have you been and what did you do there?*

Part 2

Candidate A

Teacher: I'm going to give each of you a photograph of Johannesburg. Candidate A, show the photo to the other candidates. Describe it and tell us what you think of when you think of Johannesburg? Does this picture surprise you?

Candidate B

Teacher: Candidate B, show the photo to the other candidates. Describe the picture and tell us if you would do a tour of a township in Johannesburg. Why (not)?

Candidate C

Teacher: Candidate C, show the photo to the other candidates and describe the picture. Talk about how you experienced the Football World Cup in South Africa. Did you watch the matches? Where did you watch them and what was it like?

Part 3

Teacher: Now I'd like you to have a discussion. Would you like to visit Johannesburg? What do you think is interesting about the city? What would you like to see and do?

GOST Speaking: A globalized world

Part 1

Please answer the questions about yourself.
- *Would you like to spend some time in a foreign country? Where would you like to go and why?*
- *Are you interested in meeting people from abroad? Why (not)?*
- *Is there a time in the past you would like to live in? Why?*

Part 2

Candidate A

"A Japanese company will deliver them to us for £6.75 a thousand."

Teacher: I'm going to give each of you a cartoon about globalization. Candidate A, show the photo to the other candidates and describe it. Tell us about something that you have at home that shows how globalization affects your life.

Candidate B

Teacher: Candidate B, show the cartoon to the other candidates and describe it. What is the cartoon about?

"Another Starbucks on Venus."

Teacher: Candidate C, show the cartoon to the other candidates and describe it. Do you like the cartoon? Why (not)?

Candidate C

"The internet means we can organise anti-globalisation demos across the planet."

Part 3

Teacher: Now I'd like you to have a discussion. Many companies but also many people today act globally. Discuss the advantages and disadvantages. Give examples.
You may consider the following:

- getting to know foreign cultures
- local products *vs.* products from abroad
- jobs in Germany *vs.* jobs abroad
- ...

4 Freizeit – Kultur – Tourismus

EBR Listening: At a hotel

- *Klaus Kellermann, a German engineer, is in England to do a special job for his company.*
- *You are going to hear a dialogue in the hotel.*
- *Read the statements 1–10 below first, then listen to the recording.*
- *Decide whether the statements are true or false.*
- *You will hear the recording twice.*

		true	false
1	Klaus booked his room before he arrived at the hotel.	☐	☐
2	Klaus is staying in the hotel for two nights.	☐	☐
3	The hotel wants to have his home address on the form.	☐	☐
4	The receptionist wants to know the name of his company.	☐	☐
5	Klaus's room is number 114 on the second floor.	☐	☐
6	Breakfast is from 6 a.m. to 9.30 a.m.	☐	☐
7	Klaus would like a wake-up call at 7 a.m.	☐	☐
8	Klaus will need a taxi to go to the factory.	☐	☐
9	Klaus can't eat in the hotel in the evening.	☐	☐
10	There aren't any good restaurants near the hotel.	☐	☐

FOR Listening: At a New York youth hostel

- *Some American high school students are on a class trip to New York. They have just arrived at the youth hostel.*
- *Marty Lorenzo, the hostel warden[1], is telling them about the hostel.*
- *Read the brochure below first, then listen to the recording.*
- *Complete the brochure.*
- *You will hear the recording twice.*

The New York City YOUTH HOSTEL

Corner of Amsterdam Avenue and West 103rd Street, NY

The hostel

The New York City Youth Hostel is near Central Park on the Upper West Side of New York.

The building is ______________________[1] years old.

Rooms

The hostel has bedrooms for ______________________[2] guests.

There is also a TV room, a games room, a ______________________[3] and a room where you can leave your ______________________[4].

Opening times

The hostel is open ______________________[5], seven days a week, 365 days a year.

Meals

Breakfast at the youth hostel every day is at ______________________[6].

For lunch and an evening meal there are ______________________[7] nearby.

Also at the hostel ...

- Washing machines to wash your clothes
- Internet
- You can also hire ______________________[8].

1 ***hostel warden*** *Herbergsvater*

GOST Listening: Holidays in North Wales

- *Emily is telling her best friend Becky about her holiday in North Wales.*
- *Read the questions 1–5 below first, then listen to the recording.*
- *While listening: You may take notes on an extra sheet so that you can answer the questions.*
- *After listening: Write the answers. You don't have to write complete sentences, but one word is not enough.*
- *You will hear the recording twice.*

1 When and where did Emily go on holiday in Wales? (two details)

____

____

2 What was old-fashioned about Aunt Rhiannon's house?

____

3 Why didn't Emily and her brother enjoy their time on the beach? (two details)

____

____

4 Why couldn't they stay out late in the village?

____

____

5 Why were they wet and tired after the party in the next village? (two details)

____

____

____

____

EBR Speaking: Free time activities

Part 1

Please answer the questions about yourself.
- *Which languages do you speak?*
- *How long have you been learning English?*
- *What are your hobbies?*
- *Who do you spend time with outside school?*

Part 2

Candidate A

Teacher: I'm going to give each of you a picture which shows free time activities. Candidate A, show the photo to the other candidates and describe it. Which activities do you like doing?

Candidate B

Teacher: Candidate B, show the picture to the other candidates. Describe the picture and tell us who you spend your free time with. What do you do?

Candidate C

Teacher: Candidate C, show the picture to the other candidates and describe it. Do you prefer indoor or outdoor activities?

Part 3

Teacher: Now I'd like you to have a discussion. You want to meet on Saturday afternoon and do some things together. Discuss what you want to do and agree on three activities.

FOR Speaking: A perfect holiday

Part 1

Please answer the questions about yourself.

- *What do you do in your free time?*
- *What new hobby would you like to try? Why?*
- *Where did you spend your last holiday? What did you do?*

Part 2

Teacher: I'm going to give each of you a picture which shows a different kind of holiday. Candidate A, show the photo to the other candidates and describe it. Have you done a camping tour or would you like to do one?

Candidate A

Candidate B

Teacher: Candidate B, show the picture to the other candidates. Describe the picture and tell us what your dream holiday would be like.

Teacher: Candidate C, show the picture to the other candidates and describe it. Talk about your favourite holiday so far.

Candidate C

Part 3

Teacher: Now I'd like you to have a discussion. Many teenagers take a year off after school to travel around the world. Decide whether or not you would take a year off after school to travel around the world. Discuss the pros and cons.

Zur Wiederholung findest du hier die Skills File-Seiten aus dem Schülerbuch English G 21, Band 6.

SF Listening

Was muss ich beim *Listening* beachten?

Vor dem Hören:

– Überlege, worum es in dem Hörtext gehen wird. Frag dich, was du schon über das Thema weißt.
– Lies die Aufgaben gut durch, damit du weißt, worauf du achten sollst:
  - auf die **Hauptgedanken** oder die **Kernaussage** des Textes, z. B. wenn du sagen sollst, um welches Thema es geht, oder welche Meinung der Sprecher zu dem Thema hat.
  - auf bestimmte **Details**, z. B. wenn du Namen, Uhrzeiten, Jahreszahlen heraushören sollst.
– Bereite dich darauf vor, Notizen zu machen. Leg z. B. eine Tabelle oder Liste an.

Beim Hören:

– Keine Panik! Du musst nicht alles verstehen. Konzentriere dich auf das Wesentliche. Oft werden wichtige Informationen auch wiederholt.

– Achte auf Geräusche und unterschiedliche Stimmen. Was ein Sprecher / eine Sprecherin besonders betont, das ist wichtig!

– Wenn du gezielt nach Informationen suchst, denk an die Aufgabe und lass dich von anderen Einzelheiten nicht ablenken. Aufgepasst: die Informationen, die du suchst, kommen vielleicht in einer anderen Reihenfolge vor, als du sie erwartest.

– Manche Signalwörter machen es dir leichter, den Hörtext zu verstehen:
  - Aufzählung: **and**, **another**, **too**
  - Gegensatz: **although**, **but**
  - Grund, Folge: **because**, **so**, **so that**
  - Vergleich: **larger/older/... than**, **more**, **most**
  - Reihenfolge: **before**, **after**, **then**, **next**, **later**, **when**, **at last**, **at the same time**

– Mache kurze Notizen, z. B. Anfangsbuchstaben, Symbole oder Stichworte.

Nach dem Hören:

– Vervollständige deine Notizen sofort.
– Konzentriere dich beim zweiten Hören auf das, was du beim ersten Mal nicht gut verstanden hast.

SF Taking notes

Worum geht es beim Notizenmachen?

Wenn du beim Lesen oder Zuhören Notizen machst, kannst du dich später besser an das Gehörte oder Gelesene erinnern. Das ist nützlich, wenn du etwas vortragen, nacherzählen oder einen Bericht schreiben sollst.

Wie mache ich Notizen?

In Texten oder Gesprächen gibt es immer wichtige und unwichtige Wörter. Die wichtigen Wörter werden Schlüsselwörter (**key words**) genannt, und nur diese solltest du notieren. Meist sind das Substantive und Verben, manchmal auch Adjektive oder Zahlen.

Tipp

- Verwende Ziffern (z. B. 7 statt „seven“).
- Verwende Symbole und Abkürzungen, z. B. ✔ (für „ja“) und + (für „und“) oder US für „United States“, E. für „Edward“.
  Du kannst auch eigene Symbole erfinden.
- Verwende not oder ✕ statt „doesn't“ oder „don't“.

SF Describing pictures

Wie kann ich Bilder beschreiben?

- Um zu sagen, wo genau etwas abgebildet ist, benutze:
  at the top/bottom • in the foreground/background • in the middle • on the left/right
- Diese Präpositionen sind auch hilfreich:
  behind • between • in front of • next to • under
- Um zu beschreiben, was die Personen auf dem Bild tun, benutze das **present progressive**.
  Someone is riding a horse.

Wie kann ich beschreiben, was die Personen fühlen?

Oft sollst du dich in eine Person auf einem Foto hineinversetzen und beschreiben, was sie fühlt oder denkt. Schau dir das Foto genau an und nimm dir Zeit, dir die Situation vorzustellen. Beim Formulieren helfen dir *phrases* wie:
Maybe the woman/man in the photo feels ... /is thinking about ... •
I think he/she feels/wants to/...

►►►

Manchmal sollst du dir vorstellen, was die Person getan hat, bevor das Foto gemacht wurde. Achte auf Details im Foto (Hat die Person einen Gegenstand in der Hand? Wie sieht sie aus? Was tut sie?) und überlege dir, wie es zu der im Foto gezeigten Situation gekommen sein könnte (Warum ist die Person traurig, fröhlich etc.?). Verwende die **past tenses**:
Maybe he found out that ... • Perhaps he was looking for a place to relax/...

Wenn du beschreiben sollst, was wohl als Nächstes geschehen wird bzw. was die Person danach tun wird, verwendest du die **future tenses**:
He looks as if he's going to cry/... • Maybe he'll decide to ...

SF Describing cartoons

Cartoons sind humorvolle Zeichnungen, die häufig ein aktuelles Thema aufgreifen.

Wie beschreibe ich einen Cartoon?

Bei der Beschreibung eines Cartoons gehst du zunächst vor wie bei der Beschreibung von Fotos oder anderen Zeichnungen.

1. Beschreibe die Personen oder Dinge: Was tun sie gerade? Wo befinden sie sich? usw.
   The cartoon shows ... • In the foreground/ background/... there is/are ...

2. Achte darauf, ob der Cartoon eine Bildunterschrift (*caption*), Sprechblasen oder Gedankenblasen (*speech bubbles, thought bubbles*) hat.
   In the caption it says that ...

GLOBAL WARNING

Wie analysiere ich die Aussage eines Cartoons?

1. Sag, worum es in dem Cartoon geht, welches Thema er behandelt:
   The cartoon is about ...

2. Wenn du analysierst, welche Botschaft (*message*) der Cartoon-Zeichner vermitteln möchte, solltest du alle Elemente des Cartoons noch einmal zusammen betrachten: die Zeichnung sowie die Bildunterschrift und Sprech- oder Gedankenblasen. Achte darauf, ob die Personen oder Dinge positiv oder negativ dargestellt werden. Bedenke, dass ein Cartoon auch ernste Themen humorvoll darstellt und oft stark übertreibt!
   I think the cartoon shows us that ... • The artist wants to say that ...

Manchmal sollst du Stellung zur Botschaft des Cartoons nehmen und deine eigene Meinung sagen:
I like/don't like the cartoon because ... • I think the artist is right/wrong because ...

SF Talking about charts

Welche Informationen kann ich Diagrammen (*charts*) entnehmen?

Diagramme stellen statistische Vergleiche zwischen mindestens zwei Dingen dar. Es werden entweder absolute Zahlen oder Prozentsätze miteinander verglichen.

Welche unterschiedlichen Formen von Diagrammen gibt es?

- **Bar charts (Säulendiagramme)** beschreiben häufig die Anzahl oder Größe von zwei oder mehr Dingen.
- **Pie charts (Kreis-/Tortendiagramme)** geben einen schnellen Überblick über die prozentuale Verteilung.
- **Charts (Tabellen)** ermöglichen den Vergleich unterschiedlicher Daten anhand von Zahlen und Prozentsätzen.
- **Line graphs (Kurvendiagramme)** stellen den Zusammenhang zwischen zwei zu vergleichenden Größen dar.

Wie kann ich beschreiben, was die Diagramme darstellen?

Um ein Diagramm zu beschreiben, solltest du folgende Fragen beantworten:

- **What is the chart/table/graph about?**
  The bar/pie chart is about ... • The line graph deals with ... •
  It is taken from ...
- **What does the chart/table/graph compare or show?**
  The chart/table/graph compares the size/number of ... •
  It shows the different ... • The pie chart is divided into ... slices that show ...
- **What does the chart tell you? What information does it give you?**
  ... has the largest/second largest • ... is twice/three times/... as big as ... •
  There are more than/nearly twice as many ... as there are ... •
  A huge majority/small minority/ ... • ... per cent of ...

Wenn vorhanden, solltest du Aussagen über den Zeitraum der Statistik ergänzen:
The chart is about the years ...

Tipp

Benutze das **simple past**, wenn du dich auf einen Zeitpunkt in der Vergangenheit beziehst: Over 14 million tourists from the UK visited Spain in 2008.

Benutze das **simple present**, wenn du deine Schlussfolgerungen wiedergibst:
Spain is one of the most popular countries with tourists from the UK.

Benutze das **present perfect**, wenn du dich auf einen Zeitraum beziehst, der von der Vergangenheit bis heute reicht:
How many people have visited Spain since 2008?

Countries visited by UK tourists (2008)

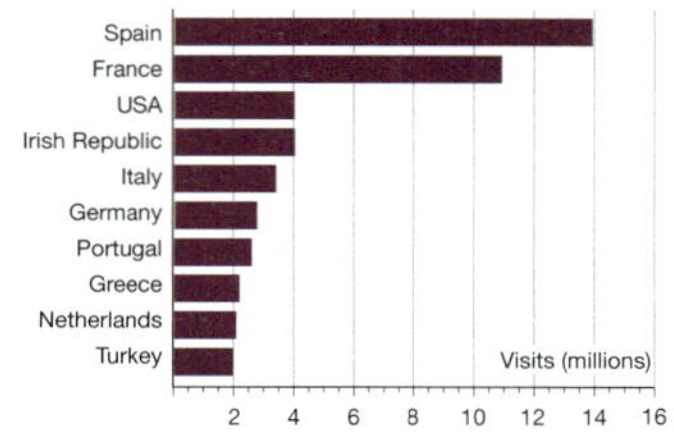

How UK citizens travelled abroad (2008)
Number of travellers:
68.9 million

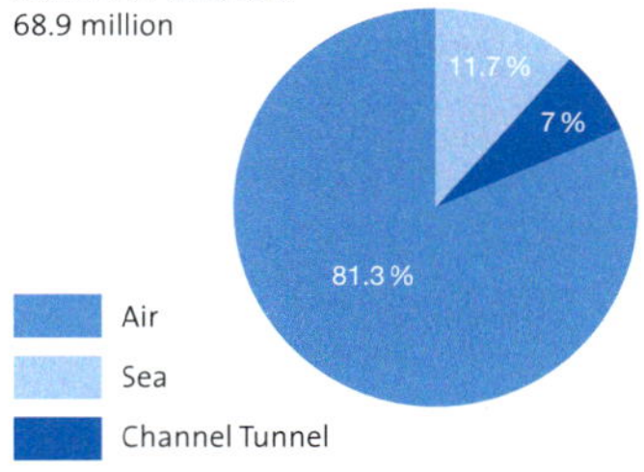

Spending by UK tourists abroad

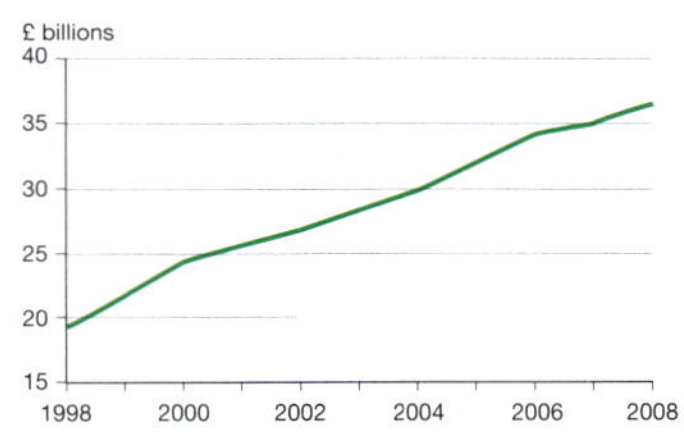

SF Having a conversation

Ein Gespräch beginnen

Ein Gespräch auf Englisch zu beginnen ist einfacher, als du vielleicht denkst. Es gibt immer mehrere Möglichkeiten:

- **Wenn du etwas erfragen willst** (z.B. den Weg oder die Uhrzeit) **oder um Hilfe bitten möchtest:**
  Excuse me, do you know ... • Excuse me, can you tell me ... • Excuse me, do you know where... • Could you help me, please?
- **Wenn du jemanden begrüßen möchtest oder kennenlernst:**
  Hi! • Hello! • Good morning. • (bei Erwachsenen) Good afternoon.
  Oft kann man das Gespräch dann mit einer allgemeinen Bemerkung weiterführen: Great day today! • Nice concert, isn't it? • ...
  Oft hört man zur Begrüßung auch How are you? oder How do you do? Das sind einfache Begrüßungsformeln, auf die keine ausführliche Antwort erwartet wird. Am besten sagst du einfach Fine, thanks. How about you?
- **Wenn du jemanden wiedertriffst:**
  Hi, ..., how are things? • Hi, how is it going? • How are you? • Hi, good to see/meet you.

Ein Gespräch führen

Für den weiteren Verlauf des Gesprächs sind diese Wendungen nützlich:

- **Sich vorstellen:** By the way, my name's ... • I'm ...
- **Sich kennen lernen:** Have you ... before? • Have you ever ...? • What about you?
- **Sich bedanken/auf Dank reagieren:** Thanks! • Thanks for your help. • You're welcome.
- **Sich verabschieden:** See you tomorrow/next week. • Bye!

Und wenn du einmal etwas nicht verstanden hast, kannst du nachfragen:
Sorry, I didn't get that. • Sorry, can you say that again, please?

SF Asking for, confirming, giving information

Ein Gespräch ist mehr als nur der Austausch von Informationen; es kommt auch auf einen höflichen und angenehmen Ton an. Das gilt natürlich auch für Gespräche auf Englisch. Diese Wendungen können hilfreich sein:

- **Asking for information:** Oft beginnt man eine Anfrage oder Auskunft mit Excuse me... • Excuse me, could you tell me, ... • Would you mind telling me ... • Sorry, I'd just like to know ... • I'm not quite sure about ... • Is it/Are they ...? • Is it right that ...? • Can I just ask ... • Excuse me, I've just got a question. • Excuse me, do you think you could ...?
- **Confirming information:** Wenn du nachfragen oder sicher gehen möchtest, dass du etwas richtig verstanden hast, kannst du das z.B. so tun: Can I just confirm ...? • Is it right that ...? • Have I got that right ...? • ..., (is that) right? • Could you just say that again, please? Auch question tags drücken den Wunsch nach Bestätigung aus: This is the library, isn't it?

Denke auch daran, dich für die erhaltenen Informationen freundlich zu bedanken.

- **Giving information:** Auch wenn du selbst eine Auskunft erteilst, versuche freundlich und höflich zu sein, z. B. mit einer kurzen Einleitung:
  Sure. • Of course, no problem. • Well, just a second. • Give me a minute to think about it.
  Wenn du nicht weiter helfen kannst, drückst du dein Bedauern aus:
  Oh, I'm sorry, I don't know. • Sorry, I'm afraid I can't help you.

SF Having a discussion

Seine Meinung sagen und erklären

- **Expressing an opinion:** In einer Diskussion ist es gut, wenn du möglichst klar und deutlich sagst, was du zu einer bestimmten Frage denkst:
  I think ... • I feel ... • In my opinion ...
- **Giving reasons and examples**: Es ist aber noch wichtiger, dass du Beispiele und Argumente nennst, die deine Meinung unterstützen – schließlich willst du deine Gesprächspartner ja überzeugen: because ... • First ... / Second ... • For example ... • Let me explain ... • That's why ...

Auf andere reagieren

- **Asking for clarification:** Manchmal ist es notwendig nachzuhaken:
  Could you say that again? • Sorry, but I don't understand what you mean.
- **Agreeing with someone:** Die Meinung eines anderen unterstützt du mit
  I agree (with you/...). • That's a good point. • You're right.
- **Disagreeing with someone:** Oft widerspricht man nicht direkt, sondern leitet seine Reaktion z. B. mit Sorry, ... ein. Zeig immer Respekt für die Meinung anderer.
  I don' t think you can say ... • I see what you mean but ... • No, that's not right. • Sorry, I don't agree with you. • Yes, but ..., • Well, I don't think you can say that ... • Ah, come on, ...

SF Paraphrasing

Worum geht es beim Paraphrasing?

Paraphrasing bedeutet, etwas mit anderen Worten zu erklären. Das ist hilfreich, wenn dir ein bestimmtes Wort nicht einfällt oder wenn dein Gegenüber dich nicht verstanden hat.

Wie gehe ich beim *Paraphrasing* vor?

- Man kann mit einem Wort umschreiben, das dieselbe Bedeutung hat:
  to train is the same as to practise
  Oder man sagt das Gegenteil: **alive is the opposite of dead**
- Manchmal braucht man mehrere Wörter, z. B. wenn man etwas beschreibt oder erklärt. Dabei benutzt man ein allgemeines Wort (**general word**) und nennt weitere Eigenschaften.
  A racing car is a very fast car.
- Oder du umschreibst das Wort mit **... is/are like ...**
  A chef is like a cook, he or she is the main cook in a restaurant.
- Du kannst auch einen Relativsatz (**relative clause**) verwenden:
  A garage is a place where cars are checked and repaired.
  A nurse is a person who looks after people who are ill, usually in a hospital.

SF Brainstorming

Wofür ist Brainstorming gut?

Bei vielen Aufgaben ist es nützlich, wenn du im ersten Schritt möglichst viele Ideen zum Thema sammelst. Dabei hilft dir das **Brainstorming**.

Wie gehe ich beim Brainstorming vor?

Schritt 1:
Schreib alle Ideen so auf, wie sie dir einfallen. Es ist zunächst völlig egal, ob sie gut sind oder nicht. Du kannst die Ideen durcheinander auf einen Zettel schreiben oder schon etwas geordnet, z. B. für jede eine neue Zeile.
Schritt 2:
Lies alle deine Ideen durch und wähle die besten aus. Dann sortiere sie und fasse sie sinnvoll zusammen. Dabei kannst du folgende **Techniken** anwenden:

1. Leg eine **Mindmap** an. Schreib das Thema in die Mitte eines Blattes Papier. Überlege, welche Oberbegriffe zu deiner Sammlung von Ideen passen. Verwende unterschiedliche Farben. Ergänze jede Idee, die zu einem Oberbegriff passt, auf einem Nebenast. Nimm dafür nur wichtige Schlüsselwörter. Du kannst statt Wörtern auch Symbole verwenden und Bilder ergänzen.
2. **The 5 Ws**: Schreib die **5 W-Fragen** **Who? What? Where? When? Why?** in eine Tabelle. Die Ideen, die dir zu jeder Frage kommen, kannst du darunter schreiben.

GOST Speaking: Learning foreign languages

Part 1

Please answer the questions about yourself.

- *What do you usually do in your holidays?*
- *Do you like learning English? Why (not)?*
- *Which language(s) would you like to learn? Why?*

Part 2

Teacher: I'm going to give each of you a picture about some kind of student exchange. Candidate A, show the picture to the other candidates and describe it. Would you like to attend a language course in a foreign country? Why (not)?

Candidate A

Candidate B

Teacher: Candidate B, show the picture to the other candidates. Describe the picture. Talk about your experiences of learning foreign languages.

Teacher: Candidate C, show the picture to the other candidates. Describe the picture and tell us if would you like to go on a student exchange to the USA. Why (not)?

Candidate C

Part 3

Teacher: Now I'd like you to have a discussion. Compare a language course at home with a language course in the country where the language is spoken. Discuss the advantages and disadvantages of each way. Here are some ideas for your discussion:

- cultural experience
- price
- time
- ...

5 Vielfalt in der Gesellschaft

EBR Listening: School report on drugs

- *You are going to hear a report on drugs at British schools.*
- *Read the questions below first, then listen to the recording.*
- *Answer the questions.*
- *You will hear the recording twice.*

1 Mark *true* or *false*.

		true	false
1	Pupils start smoking or drinking alcohol when they are sixteen.	☐	☐
2	Many pupils think smoking is cool.	☐	☐
3	All pupils know that smoking or drinking alcohol is dangerous.	☐	☐
4	If pupils smoke, they may have to leave school.	☐	☐

2 Tick (✓) the right answer A, B or C.

1 When pupils start smoking or drinking alcohol they
A ☐ think about the consequences.
B ☐ don't think about the consequences.
C ☐ mustn't think about the consequences.

2 The longer you smoke,
A ☐ the more difficult it becomes to stop.
B ☐ the easier it becomes to stop.
C ☐ the better it tastes.

3 Smoking at school often gives pupils
A ☐ a bad feeling.
B ☐ a chance to relax.
C ☐ an 'extra kick'.

4 Some schools now even
A ☐ lock the toilets.
B ☐ block the toilets.
C ☐ have no toilets.

FOR Listening: Emotions

- *You are going to hear five people talking about emotions.*
- *Read the statements A–F below first, then listen to the recording.*
- *Choose the correct statement for each person.*
- *There is one statement that you don't need.*
- *Write the correct letters in the spaces.*
- *You will hear the recording twice.*

A Sport can help you to deal with your anger.

B Crying is healthy.

C 'Road rage' is when drivers get angry and aggressive.

D Crying and laughing are equally important.

E People in the country show their emotions more than people in the city.

F Showing anger and aggression is often a way of hiding other emotions.

Person	Statement
Rebecca	
Emmie	
Daniel	
Ryan	
Adam	

GOST Listening: It's cool to say "No"

- *Two students are being interviewed on the radio about how they started smoking and how they managed to stop.*
- *Read the questions below first, then listen to the recording.*
- *Answer the questions.*
- *You will hear the recording twice.*

1 Mark *true* or *false*.

		true	false
1	Karen and Chris stopped smoking before it was too late.	☐	☐
2	Karen and Chris are university students.	☐	☐
3	Chris asked a friend to give him his first cigarette.	☐	☐
4	Chris enjoyed the taste of his first cigarette.	☐	☐
5	Karen smoked her first cigarette because she wanted to be like the other girls.	☐	☐

2 Complete the statements.

1 Chris thought if he wanted to be part of the gang, he ______________________.

2 Karen had a cigarette whenever she felt ______________________.

3 It's easy to get cigarettes from ______________________.

4 Karen spent all her ______________________.

5 Karen feels bad about ______________________ her parents.

3 Are the statements true for Chris or for Karen? Mark each statement with C (Chris) or K (Karen).

1 A teacher helped him/her to break his/her smoking habit. ☐

2 He/She found it really hard to stop smoking. ☐

3 When he/she gave up smoking, he/she also gave up some friends. ☐

EBR Speaking: Bullying

Part 1

Please answer the questions about yourself.
- *Who is your best friend? Why?*
- *Which holidays do you and your family celebrate? Which one is your favourite?*
- *What did you do yesterday evening?*

Part 2

Candidate A

Useful vocabulary:

bullying *Mobbing*

Teacher: I'm going to give each of you a photo about bullying. Candidate A, show the photo to the other candidates and describe it. Have you heard of someone who was or is being bullied, e.g. a friend or someone in the news? What happened?

Candidate B

Teacher: Candidate B, show the photo to the other candidates and describe it. What do you think are the girls in the background saying to the girl in the foreground? How do you think the girl in the foreground feels?

Candidate C

Teacher: Candidate C, show the photo to the other candidates and describe it. Have you seen a fight? What happened?

Part 3

Teacher: Now I'd like you to have a discussion. What would you suggest to a friend who has a problem with bullying? Should this friend tell anyone? Would you tell anyone? Where and how can this friend get help?

FOR Speaking: **Getting involved**

Part 1

Please answer the questions about yourself.
- *What do you usually do at the weekends?*
- *What's your favourite holiday? Why?*
- *Have you ever had a fight with a friend or someone in your family? What was it about?*

Part 2

Candidate A

Useful vocabulary:

bullying *Mobbing*

Teacher: I'm going to give each of you a photo about bullying. Candidate A, show the photo to the other candidates and describe it. Tell us if you would help the boy in the photo.

Candidate B

Teacher: Candidate B, show the photo to the other candidates and describe it. Talk about other forms of bullying you know.

Candidate C

Teacher: Candidate C, show the photo to the other candidates and describe it. What situation are these teenagers in?

Part 3

Teacher: Now I'd like you to have a discussion. Imagine the following situation: You see teenagers in the street who are bullying another teenager. Discuss whether or not you want to help that teenager.

GOST Speaking: Drugs

Part 1

Please answer the questions about yourself.
- *What will you do this afternoon?*
- *What do you like about your family?*
- *Would you describe yourself as a traditional person? Why (not)?*

Part 2

Candidate A

Teacher: I'm going to give each of you a photograph which shows teenagers using drugs. Candidate A, show the photo to the other candidates. Describe it and talk about the habit of smoking among your friends or family.

Candidate B

Teacher: Candidate B, show the photo to the other candidates and describe it. What are the risks when drinking alcohol?

Teacher: Candidate C, show the photo to the other candidates and describe it. Talk about the problems taking drugs can cause.

Candidate C

Part 3

Teacher: Now I'd like you to have a discussion. What are the reasons why teenagers start smoking, drinking or taking drugs? Give examples.

6 Mensch und Natur

EBR Listening: What will the future look like?

- *On a radio programme two scientists, Professor Jones and Professor Miller, are discussing the future.*
- *Read the questions below first and look at the useful vocabulary. Then listen to the recording.*
- *Answer the questions.*
- *You will hear the recording twice.*

Useful vocabulary:

power line	*Hochspannungsleitung*
to develop	*entwickeln*
produce	*produzieren*

1 Tick (✓) the correct answer: A, B, or C.

1 The interview is about
A ☐ energy.
B ☐ professors.
C ☐ sunshine.

2 Professor Jones thinks that in the future
A ☐ we won't have to work any more.
B ☐ we won't have bikes any more.
C ☐ we won't have cars any more.

3 Professor Miller thinks that
A ☐ we can have electric cars.
B ☐ we can have cheaper cars.
C ☐ we can take the train.

4 You can produce electricity from
A ☐ the sun.
B ☐ electric cars.
C ☐ old bottles.

5 There is enough sunshine in
A ☐ Britain.
B ☐ Africa.
C ☐ Ireland.

6 The problem with long power lines is that
A ☐ they look ugly.
B ☐ you lose too much energy.
C ☐ they are too expensive.

2 Complete the sentences according to the text. Choose words from the box. Be careful – not all of them are correct.

the environment | car | bike | electricity | oil | bottles | changes for everybody | sunshine

1 If there is no more oil left, it will mean big ______________________ .

2 Without cars, people will have to go by ______________________ .

3 Of course you can't transport electricity in ______________________ .

4 Professor Miller thinks that we can save ______________________ .

FOR Listening: The history of modern technology

- *You are going to hear Mr Kowalski, an American high school teacher, talking to his science class about modern technology.*
- *Read the statements 1–10 below first, then listen to the recording.*
- *Decide whether the statements are true or false.*
- *You will hear the recording twice.*

		true	false
1	Mr Kowalski begins by showing the class a photo on a projector.	☐	☐
2	One of the students, Luis, makes a joke about the photo.	☐	☐
3	Mr Kowalski was two years old in 1969.	☐	☐
4	The first colour TVs were made in 1955.	☐	☐
5	The Kowlaski family had a colour TV.	☐	☐
6	There were no PCs (small home computers) or pocket calculators in 1969.	☐	☐
7	The world wide web was started by an American scientist called Tim Berners-Lee in 1990.	☐	☐
8	The girl heard a programme on the radio about the world wide web.	☐	☐
9	Cell phones, CDs and PCs all appeared in the same year.	☐	☐
10	The class ends when Mr Kowalski stops talking.	☐	☐

GOST Listening: Stress

- *You are going to hear Grace and Tom from the Stress Society.*
- *They are talking about the problem of stress.*
- *Read the questions below first, then listen to the recording.*
- *Answer the questions.*
- *You will hear the recording twice.*

1 Mark *true* or *false*.

		true	false
1	Your feelings about a situation can cause stress.	☐	☐
2	According to Grace there are two ways to deal with stress.	☐	☐
3	If you choose the 'flight' route, you deal with your problems.	☐	☐
4	People who have stress also have high blood pressure.	☐	☐
5	If you suffer from mood swings you might suffer from stress.	☐	☐
6	Sugar and caffeine can influence your stress chemicals.	☐	☐

2 Complete the sentences.

1 Two of the signs of stress that Tom and Grace mention are ____________________

and ____________________ .

2 Healthy ways to cope with stress are ____________________ , your diet

and ____________________ .

3 If you suffer from stress you should ____________________ e.g. your parents or

a teacher. You shouldn't ____________________ .

EBR Speaking: A healthy lifestyle

Part 1

Please answer the questions about yourself.
- *What's your favourite food?*
- *What's your favourite sport?*
- *What's your favourite animal?*

Part 2

Teacher: I'm going to give each of you a picture which shows teenagers in different situations. Candidate A, show the picture to the other candidates and describe it. Do you like going to fast food restaurants?

Candidate A

Candidate B

Teacher: Candidate B, show the picture to the other candidates. Describe it and talk about what you do to have a healthy lifestyle.

Candidate C

Teacher: Candidate C, show the picture to the other candidates and describe it. Do you cook at home or do you meet friends to cook together? What do you cook?

Part 3

Teacher: I'm going to describe a situation to you. A friend of yours wants to have a healthier lifestyle. Agree on suggestions you can give him/her. Here are some pictures to give you ideas.

FOR Speaking: Different ways of living

Part 1

Please answer the questions about yourself.
- *Do you do any sport? Where and how often do you do it?*
- *What kind of sport do you like? Why?*
- *Do you like your hometown or village? What do you like best about it?*

Part 2

Candidate A

Teacher: I'm going to give each of you a photograph which shows a different place. Candidate A, show the photograph to the other candidates and describe it. What do you think life in a big city is like?

Candidate B

Teacher: Candidate B, show the photograph to the other candidates. Describe it and talk about the town or village you are from.

Teacher: Candidate C, show the photograph to the other candidates and describe it. Where is your ideal place to live?

Candidate C

Part 3

Teacher: Now I'd like you to have a discussion. The photographs show different places – a big city, a small quiet town or a village. Discuss the advantages and disadvantages of living at each type of place.

GOST Speaking: Natural disasters

Part 1

Please answer the questions about yourself.

- *What do you like about the place you come from? Why?*
- *Do you protect the environment? How?*
- *Do you try to have a healthy lifestyle? What do you do?*

Part 2

Candidate A

Teacher: I'm going to give each of you a photograph which shows a natural disaster. Candidate A, show the photograph to the other candidates and describe it. What would you do if you were one of the people in the picture?

Candidate B

Teacher: Candidate B, show the photograph to the other candidates and describe it. Have you ever experienced extreme weather? What was it like?

Teacher: Candidate C, show the photograph to the other candidates and describe it. Talk about natural disasters you have heard of in the news recently.

Candidate C

Part 3

Teacher: Now I'd like you to have a discussion. Many scientists say that the number of hurricanes is growing. They say the reason for this is global warming. Discuss this statement. Give reasons for your opinion.

7 Medien in der Gesellschaft

EBR Listening: The media

- *You are going to hear five people talking about the media.*
- *Read the statements A–F below first, then listen to the recording.*
- *Choose the correct statement for each person.*
- *There is one statement that you don't need.*
- *Write the correct letters in the spaces.*
- *You will hear the recording twice.*

A We are lucky to have so many different ways of getting entertainment and information.

B Most people are influenced by the media.

C You can do other things while you are listening to the radio.

D You can get more information from newspapers than from TV or radio.

E TV programmes could be better.

F The cinema isn't cheap but it's great!

Person	Statement
Mark	
Marion	
Dean	
Richie	
Andrea	

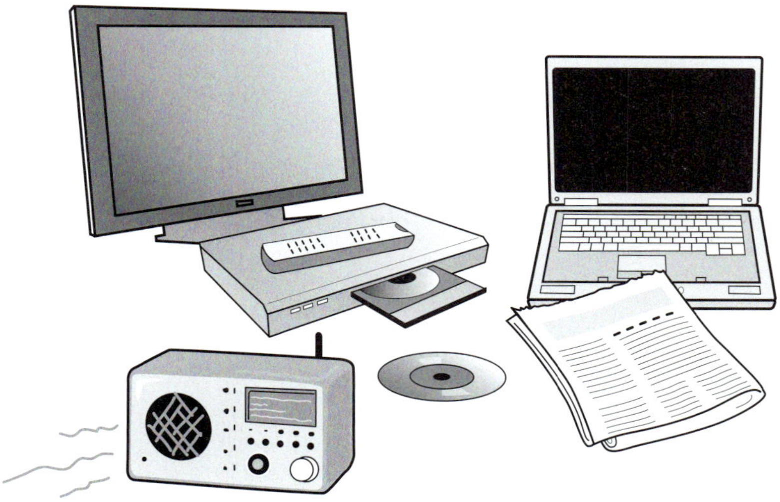

FOR Listening: An internet summer camp

- *You are going to hear part of a radio programme from Australia.*
- *Read the statements 1–7 below first and look at the useful vocabulary. Then listen to the recording.*
- *Tick (✓) the correct answer: A, B or C.*
- *You will hear the recording twice.*

1 The summer camp lasts

A ☐ two weeks.
B ☐ three weeks.
C ☐ four weeks.

2 The camp is for young people who

A ☐ don't have a computer at home.
B ☐ want to learn how to use the internet.
C ☐ spend too long on the internet.

3 The camp is the idea of

A ☐ the Australian government.
B ☐ the teenagers' parents.
C ☐ the teenagers' schools.

4 At the weekend, Linda says she is often online

A ☐ four hours a day.
B ☐ all day.
C ☐ 12 hours or more.

5 When she's online, Linda mostly

A ☐ chats to friends in Australia.
B ☐ chats to friends in different countries.
C ☐ chats to her school friends.

6 Linda decided to come to the camp because

A ☐ she read about it in a newspaper.
B ☐ her teacher at school said it was a good idea.
C ☐ her parents said it was a good idea.

7 Linda says the first week at the camp

A ☐ was hard, but now she finds it easier.
B ☐ was easy, but now she finds it hard.
C ☐ was hard and now she finds it even harder.

Useful vocabulary:

internet addict *Internetsüchtige(r)*

GOST Listening: A media use survey

- *You are going to hear a street interview. The interviewer is doing a survey about how young people in the UK use different media.*
- *Read the questionnaire below first, then listen to the recording.*
- *Complete the questionnaire. You don't have to write full sentences.*
- *You will hear the recording twice.*

MEDIA USE SURVEY

1 How often do you listen to the radio?

A ☐ every day

B ☒ often (e. g. 2–3 times a week)

C ☐ sometimes (e. g. 2–3 times a month)

D ☐ never

2 What do you listen to most often on radio (e. g. news)?

breakfast show

3 Roughly how many hours of TV do you watch in a typical week?

☐ 0–3 ☐ 4–6 ☒ 7–9 ☐ 10+

4 Which of the following types of programmes do you often watch on TV?

☐ sport ☐ news ☐ comedy ☐ soaps

☐ documentary ☐ drama ☐ science ☐ quizzes

5 Roughly how many hours do you spend on the internet in a typical week?

☐ 0–3 ☐ 4–6 ☐ 7–9 ☐ 10+

6 Which of the following do you do on the internet?

A ☐ send emails
B ☐ chat with Instant Messages
C ☐ use an internet telephone (e. g. Skype)
D ☐ do research (e. g. for studies, business)
E ☐ read news
F ☐ shop
G ☐ listen to or download music

Which **two** of the above activities would you say are the most important to you?

....

7 How often do you read a newspaper?

....

8 Do you ever read magazines?

A ☐ No
B ☐ If yes: what kind of magazine do you read? (e. g. sports)

....

9 How often do you go to the cinema?

☐ about once a week ☐ more than once a week ☐ less than once a week

10 Do you watch films other than at the cinema?

A ☐ No
B ☐ If yes, how do you watch films (e. g. do you rent or buy DVDs?)

....

11 I'd like to ask you two general questions about how you use different media.

A Which of the different media we have talked about would you say is your main source of news?

....

B Do you think that your use of different media now is different from two years ago? If so, what has changed most in the last two years?

....

....

AGE .... **GENDER** ☐ Male ☐ Female

OCCUPATION ....

EBR Speaking: Electronic lives

Part 1

Please answer the questions about yourself.

- *What's your favourite film?*
- *Who is your favourite singer or band?*
- *Do you have a mobile phone? How often do you use it?*

Part 2

Candidate A

Teacher: I'm going to give each of you a photograph which shows teenagers using different kinds of media. Candidate A, show the photograph to the other candidates and describe it. What kind of media do you use?

Candidate B

Teacher: Candidate B, show the photograph to the other candidates and describe it. Do you play video games?

Candidate C

Teacher: Candidate C, show the picture to the other candidates and describe it. Tell us what you use the internet for.

Part 3

Teacher: Now I'd like you to have a discussion. The majority of households in Germany use the internet. Discuss the advantages and disadvantages of using the internet.

FOR Speaking: Social networking sites

Part 1

Please answer the questions about yourself.

- *What's your favourite book? Why?*
- *What was an exciting or great event you went to? Why was it exciting or great?*
- *How much time a day do you spend on the internet? What do you use the internet for?*

Part 2

Candidate A

Teacher: I'm going to give each of you a cartoon which shows users of social networking sites. Candidate A, show the cartoon to the other candidates and describe it. What's your attitude towards social networking sites?

Candidate B

"Sorry - I'd love to come out, but I'm busy updating my Facebook status."

Teacher: Candidate B, show the cartoon to the other candidates and describe it. Talk about the problem the cartoon describes.

Candidate C

"When I asked you to read a book, I didn't mean Facebook."

Teacher: Candidate C, show the cartoon to the other candidates and describe it. Could you be the boy in the cartoon? Why (not)?

Part 3

Teacher: Now I'd like you to have a discussion. Many people use social networking sites and post lots of personal information on the internet. What are the advantages of using a social networking site? What are the risks? Are there any disadvantages if you don't use a social networking site?

GOST Speaking: Media use

Part 1

Please answer the questions about yourself.
- *What kind of films do you like? Why?*
- *What kind of music do you like? Why?*
- *Do you have a mobile phone? What do you use it for?*

Part 2

Candidate A

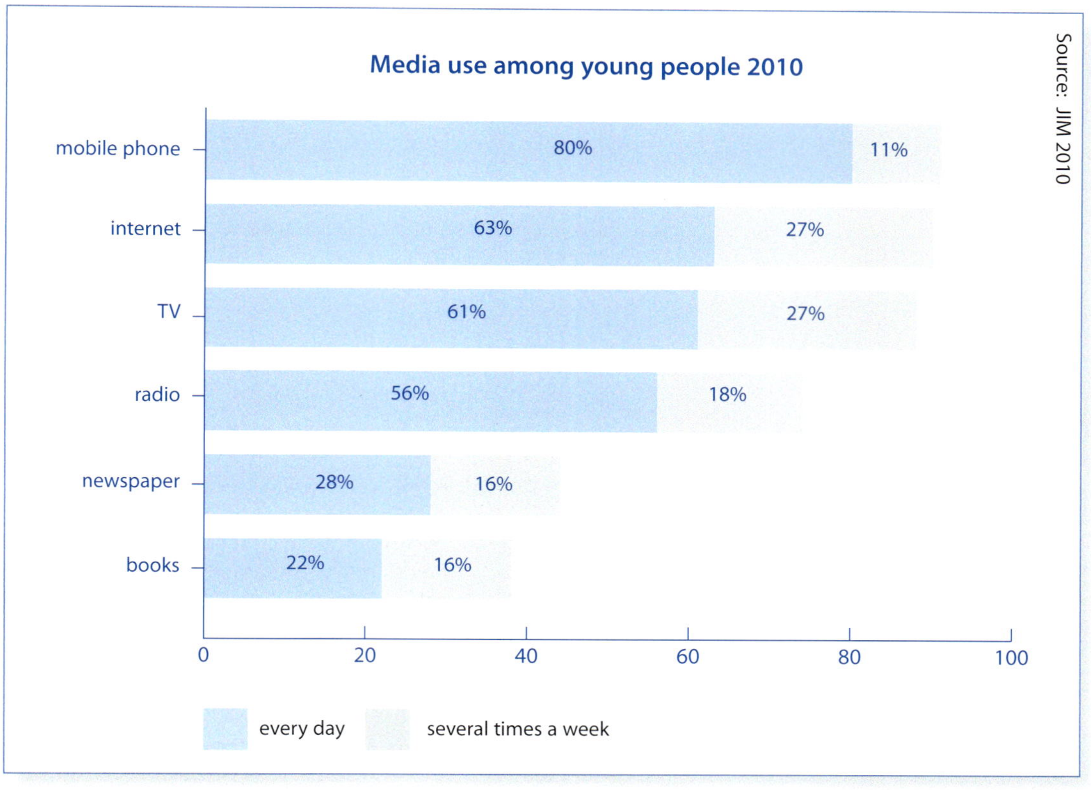

Teacher: I'm going to give each of you a chart about media and media use. Candidate A, show the chart to the other candidates and describe it. What kind of media do you use? Compare with the chart.

Teacher: Candidate B, show the chart to the other candidates. Describe it and talk about the electronic devices you have at home? Compare with the graph.

Candidate B

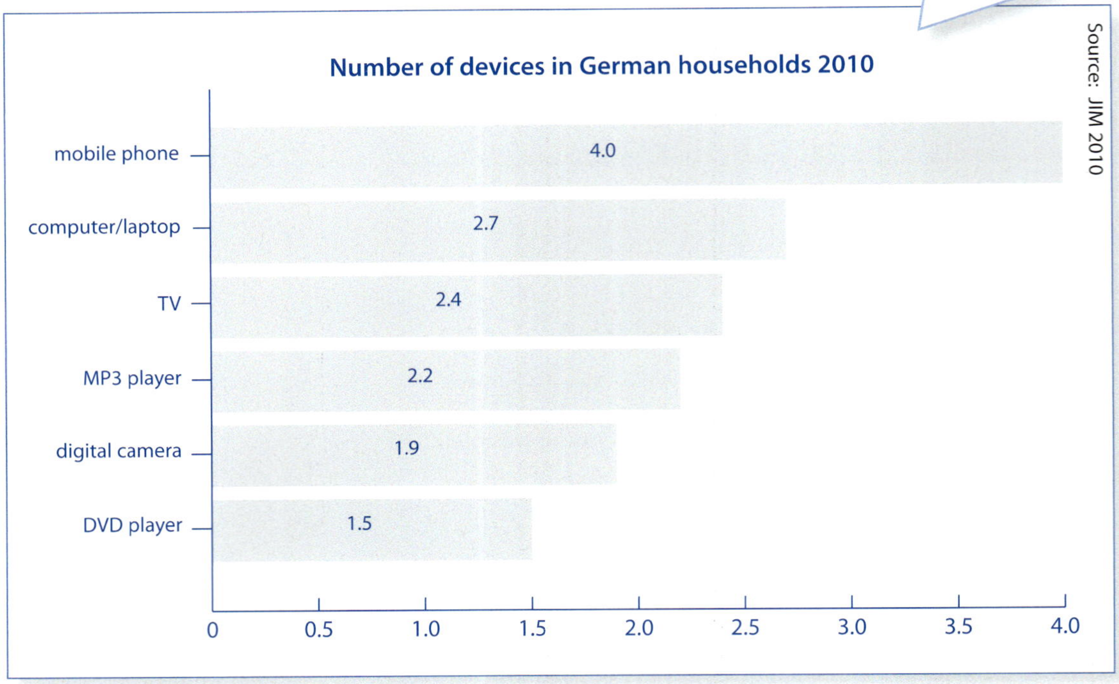

Candidate C

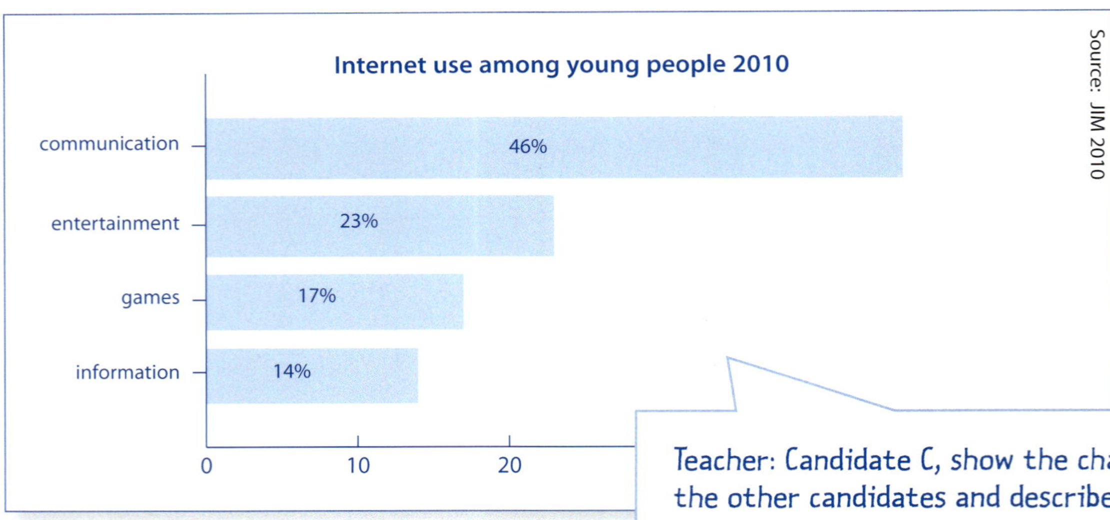

Teacher: Candidate C, show the chart to the other candidates and describe it. Tell us what you use the internet for. Compare with the graph.

Part 3

Teacher: Now I'd like you to have a discussion. There is a broad choice of media today. Discuss if the increased amount of media we use has made life easier or more difficult. Give reasons.

8 Alltag und Arbeitswelt

EBR Listening: A job interview

- *Two friends, Susan and Mohammed, are talking about Mohammed's job interview.*
- *Read the questions below first, then listen to the recording.*
- *Answer the questions.*
- *You will hear the recording twice.*

1 Mark *true* or *false*.

		true	false
1	There were three people interviewing Mohammed.	☐	☐
2	The interviewers were very impressed by his work experience.	☐	☐
3	H&M's fashion shop does not open on Saturdays.	☐	☐
4	Mohammed was happy with the money they offered him.	☐	☐

2 Tick (✓) the correct answer: A, B or C.

1 Mohammed's work experience is
- A ☐ running his own kebab shop.
- B ☐ helping in his father's kebab shop.
- C ☐ helping in his brother's kebab shop.

2 Mohammed said
- A ☐ it was OK for him to work long hours.
- B ☐ it was not OK for him to work long hours.
- C ☐ he could work late on Mondays, Wednesdays and Fridays.

3 H&M's fashion shop wanted to pay
- A ☐ 900 pounds per month.
- B ☐ 1200 pounds per month.
- C ☐ 900 pounds per year.

4 At the end of the interview,
- A ☐ Mohammed rang his brother.
- B ☐ Mohammed's brother gave him a ring.
- C ☐ Mohammed left his mobile behind.

3 Mohammed hat in seinem Vorstellungsgespräch offensichtlich ein paar Dinge falsch gemacht. Kannst du zwei davon nennen? Schreibe vollständige englische Sätze.

1 ______________________________

______________________________.

2 ______________________________

______________________________.

FOR Listening: Horrible jobs

- *You are going to hear three people, Peter, Jill and Adil, talking about horrible jobs.*
- *Read the statements 1–10 below first and look at the useful vocabulary. Then listen to the recording.*
- *Tick (✓) the correct box or complete the sentence.*
- *You will hear the recording twice.*

1 The worst kind of job Peter can imagine is

A ☐ a boring job.
B ☐ a dangerous job.
C ☐ a dirty job.

2 The three most dangerous jobs in America are woodcutter,

____

and ___________________________.

3 Adil wonders

A ☐ who makes burgers for a living.
B ☐ who kills animals for a living.
C ☐ who makes chicken soup for a living.

4 Which one of the speakers doesn't eat meat?

A ☐ Adil
B ☐ Jill
C ☐ Peter

5 Adil talks about dirty jobs such as working

in a ___________________________.

6 Peter talks about a factory that produces

A ☐ blue cheese dip.
B ☐ chicken wings.
C ☐ burgers.

7 Peter heard about the factory

A ☐ on the radio.
B ☐ in the newspaper.
C ☐ on TV.

8 What did Adil find disgusting about his job in the restaurant kitchen?

A ☐ The low pay.
B ☐ The bin of leftover food.
C ☐ The accident he had with the knives and forks.

9 Peter found his job as nightwatchman boring because he had

____

and ___________________________.

10 Jill found her telephone job frustrating because

A ☐ people didn't answer the phone.
B ☐ she often got the wrong number.
C ☐ people hung up on her.

Useful vocabulary:

woodcutter *Holzfäller*
death rate *Sterberate*
disgusting *ekelhaft*
watchman *Wächter*

GOST Listening: Life as a female FBI special agent

- *You are going to hear an interview with Candice DeLong, who worked for the FBI and wrote a book called* Special Agent.
- *Read tasks 1–6 below first, then listen to the recording.*
- *Tick (✓) the correct answer: A, B or C.*
- *You will hear the recording twice.*

1 Before becoming a special agent Candice

A ☐ worked as a doctor.

B ☐ helped mentally ill people.

C ☐ worked as a social worker.

2 Up to the 1970s

A ☐ only men worked for the FBI.

B ☐ training at the FBI was excellent.

C ☐ it was dangerous for women to fight a man.

3 Her male colleagues didn't cause her any problems because

A ☐ she hadn't grown up with sisters.

B ☐ she was better than the other agents.

C ☐ she had learned to use a weapon.

4 As part of her job

A ☐ Candice had to marry a gangster.

B ☐ Candice had to fire her gun more than once.

C ☐ Candice had to risk her life more than once.

5 Candice thinks her job at the FBI

A ☐ was too risky.

B ☐ was like an exciting movie.

C ☐ wasn't always enjoyable.

6 Her book and her TV series were successful

A ☐ in Europe and the United States.

B ☐ in her own country.

C ☐ all over the world.

EBR Speaking: The working world

Part 1

Please answer the questions about yourself.
- *Do you have a job besides school? What do you do?*
- *Have you ever done practical training in a company? Where did you do it?*
- *What did you do yesterday?*

Part 2

Candidate A

Useful vocabulary:

flight attendant *Flugbegleiter/in*

Teacher: I'm going to give each of you a photo of someone doing a job. Candidate A, show the photo to the other candidates and describe it. Would you like to work as a flight attendant?

Candidate B

Useful vocabulary:

zoo keeper Tierwärter/in

Teacher: Candidate B, show the photo to the other candidates. Describe it and talk about good and bad things about being a zoo keeper.

Candidate C

Teacher: Candidate C, show the photo to the other candidates. Describe it and tell us if you would do an office job.

Part 3

Teacher: Now I'd like you to have a discussion. Your photographs show people doing very different kinds of jobs. What kind of job would you like to have one day. Discuss what's important when doing a job.

FOR Speaking: Jobs and language

Part 1

Please answer the questions about yourself.

- *Does your mum/dad/brother/sister/... work? What do they do?*
- *Do you know anyone whose job you really like? Why do you like that job?*
- *Do you help your parents at home? What do you do?*

Part 2

Candidate A

Teacher: I'm going to give each of you a photo of someone doing a job. Candidate A, show the photo to the other candidates and describe it. What do you think is interesting about the tourist guide's job? What is not interesting?

Candidate B

Teacher: Candidate B, show the photo to the other candidates and describe it. What do you think these men's normal working days look like?

Teacher: Candidate C, show the photo to the other candidates and describe it. What do you think the waiters feel like in their job?

Candidate C

Part 3

Teacher: Now I'd like you to have a discussion. You have the opportunity of getting an apprenticeship and later a job abroad. Discuss the advantages and disadvantages of training and working in a foreign country.

GOST Speaking: Women in the job market

Part 1

Please answer the questions about yourself.

- *What does your perfect day look like? What would you do?*
- *Which job would you like to do one day? Why?*
- *Would you go abroad for a job? Why (not)?*

Part 2

Teacher: I'm going to give each of you a photo of women in their jobs. Candidate A, show the photo to the other candidates and describe it. Do you think that there are still jobs which are typical for men and women? Why (not)?

Candidate A

Candidate B

Teacher: Candidate B, show the photo to the other candidates and describe it. Tell us what you think about women in high positions.

Candidate C

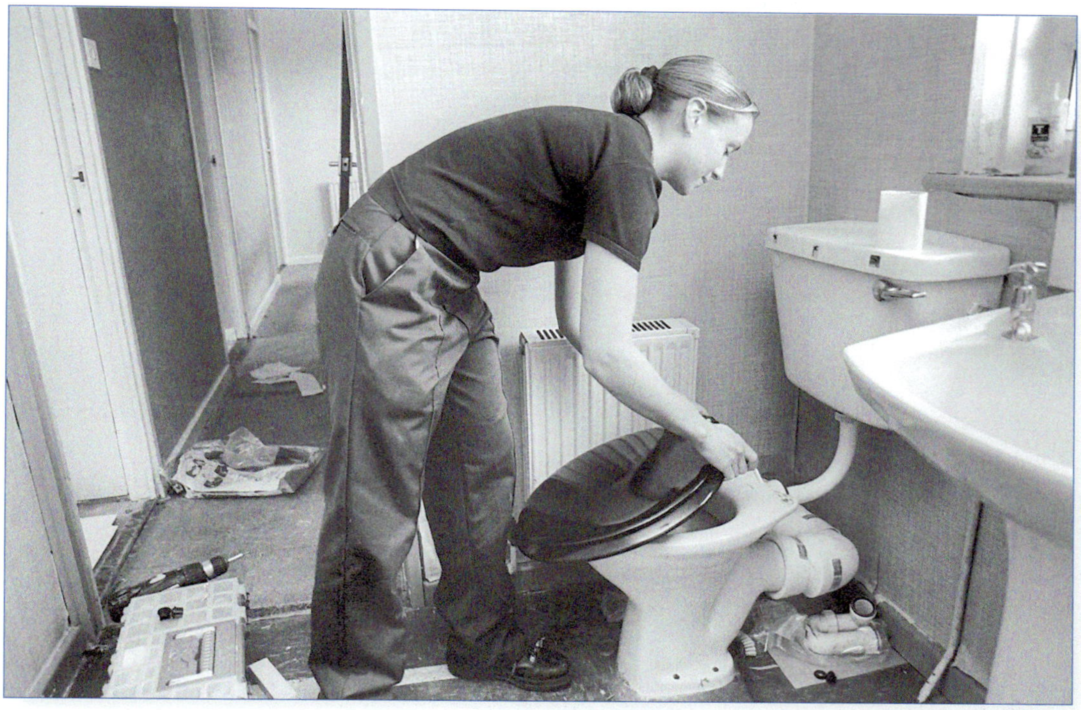

Teacher: Candidate C, show the photo to the other candidates and describe it. Would you give up your job to care for your family? Why (not)?

Part 3

Teacher: Now I'd like you to have a discussion. Are men and women in Germany treated equally in their working life? Give reasons and examples.

NOTES